ISBN: 978-1-9161741-4-6 (soft cover)

Designed by Janey Mcleod-White, Positive Poetry

info@positivepoetry.org

A Little Book of Doggerel

Written by Gail Halley

Illustrated by Sue McLeod

Thank God for Dogs!

And for the encouragement from friends and family, especially Mark and Sue Stephens, Hilary Field and our Norwich writing group (Biddy, Anita and Letitia).

For Sue McLeod whose lovely illustrations breathed life into a project which promised neither fame nor fortune!

And for all the help from Sue and Mike's daughters, Janey founder of Positive Poetry who has bravely taken on publishing our efforts, and Sarah for all her help with layout and technological input.

Remembering Solo
who made me
laugh everyday

And for Millie who
still does

And for all the lovely foster dogs from Dogs' Trust
Snetterton, a few of whom feature in these verses – along
with the Snetterton staff who care for them.

Poems

1   Terriers

6   Spaniels

11   Greyhound

15   Golden Retriever

19   Sealyham

21   To a Young Dog

23   Little Old Dog

25   Two Old Gents

27   Not Going for a Walkie
      with Corkey the Yorkie

31   Labrador

35   Where are the Poodles?

37   Charlie, Freddy & Bill

43   Little Dog Leaping in the Long Grass

51   Poor Little Rich Dog

54   To a Sleeping Tibetan Terrier

Puppy

57   The Other Side of Dolly

61   Boxer

65   Parson Jack Russell

67   How Those Dogs Move!

69   Milly Sniffalot & Molly

Scoffalot

73   Chart Topper – Le Bulldog

75   My Collie, My Lovely

77   Glen

81   The Good, The Bad & The

Restoration

85   Farewell

Terriers

Great big dog
in a small small skin
Bright as a button
Sharp as a pin

Where shall we go?
What shall we do?

Just show us the drill
We're in for the kill
We don't do sitting still.

Big big dog
in a little small skin,
Looking out for trouble,
'Trouble, let me in!'

Where shall we go?
What shall we do?

New places to enjoy
New people to annoy
We always have a ploy.

Little wee dog in his own
small skin
Tight upon my lap
Paws curled under chin.

Where do you go
In your lively little dreams?

Chasing rabbits through the
night
Seeking where to pick a fight
Waking in the early light

Big dog again,
'World, count me in!'
Giant of a dog
In his little small skin

Spaniels

Springer, Sussex, working Cocker,
Clumber, Cavalier or Sprocker,

Spaniels come in many guises,
Colours, temperaments and sizes,

But one thing makes them all such
dears
And that's the wonder of their ears:

Spaniel pups like baby goats
Leap and frolic, ears like wings;

Working cockers, full of drive
Sniff out drugs or flush out game;
And now it seems they're finding
fame
In scenting tumours, saving lives.

When springers spring, their
ears take flight

While cavaliers – such gentle
souls –
Trail their ears in feeding
bowls
But seldom bicker, snarl or
fight.
With those ears as their
trademark,
Life with spaniels is a lark.
Grooming them can be a
chore
With mud on belly, tail and
paw,
But isn't that what we are
for?

Greyhound

Born to run and hunt and kill
And leave all others standing still

        Bred to pound along the track
        Ears flattened, never looking back

The greyhound is a speed machine
Swift, sinewy and ribcage lean...

     Then,
     beaten by upstarts and so they called time
     On this muscled-up dog who was still in his prime.

Now,
Who will want him and what is his worth?
Just three years old and brimming with life
All he has known since the day of his birth

Snatched from him,

gone like the blink of an eye.

Companion dog? Household pet?

It's quite preposterous .... and yet

......?

SDM 2020

Still he can run – but now at leisure

Six times round the field – sheer pleasure.

And then to return, as companion dogs do
To rest his long limbs where it's cosy and warm,
Stretched end to end on a sofa for two
Elegant paw draped on silk-covered arm.

The long supple body which stretched down the
track
Has learnt to stretch up and has found out the
knack of taking the food that was hidden from
sight,
But not from the reach of a greyhound's great
height.

And so five stone of muscle and sinew and strength
Yawns, sees the snow and gives a slight shiver,
Then settles once more and stretches full length
And dreams not of racetracks
but platefuls of liver.

Golden Retriever

Gentle joyful jolly Goldie
Full of smiles, she rolls to greet you
Waving her tail she seems to say
'It's always a pleasure to meet you'.

Life is not too serious
Life's for play and friends and fun
But she'll surprise you when at work
Leading the blind or next to the gun.

She's happiest bumbling
round in the field,
But show her a puddle, a
pond or a mere
She's gone in a flash
and despite all my calls
This most obliging of dogs just
won't hear!

But she's always there when
I'm feeling low,
To cheer me or make me smile,
She's guaranteed to lighten
my life
And go with me for the
second mile.

Sealyham

Ten inches at the shoulder
Nine kilos on the scale
And half a ton of willpower
Packed in 'twixt nose and tail.

She may be small in stature
But her strength of will abounds,
And her demeanour always says,
'You can't push me around!'

Funny, clever, resolute,
She makes me laugh each day,
Though you cannot twist her arm,
And she usually gets her way.

If you're looking for slavish
devotion,
The Sealyham isn't for you
But if you seek fun and
sometimes commotion
The best of companions, a heart
that is true,

Then these squat little natural
comics
Will delight you their whole
life through.

To a Young Dog

One day you'll be an old old dog
Short of breath and stiff of limb,
With muffled ears and rheumy eyes,
Sight and hearing growing dim

But now, you're still a young young dog
Ready to run and jump and play
And chase your friends in a frenzied whirl
Every minute of every day.

And then you will be middle-aged,
Still full of beans and bounce and fun,
But happy to drop in a deep deep sleep
And dream your dreams when the day is done

And when you are an old old dog,
And can no longer run and play,
I will love you even more
And treasure each remaining day.

Little Old Dog

Little old dog, full of
lumps and bumps
Coat like a well-worn rug.
Sometimes scowly, often
growly,
"Don't disturb me – I'm
quite snug."
Little old dog with
yellowing teeth,
Unwilling to come for a jog
Not always happy, quite
often snappy,
"Put me down; I'm not a
lapdog."
Little old crosspatch,
snoring on the sofa,
The noise goes on and on,
But grumpy, bumpy, fatty-
lumpy,
I'll be gutted when you've
gone.

Two Old Gents

Two old gents walk stiff and slow
As if their joints need oiling
They make their way along the path,
Less like leisure, more like toiling.

They walk together side by side,
Two old friends who've shared long years,
The two-legged one had tended sheep,
The four-legged one his eyes and ears.

I watch them nearly every day
With warmth, affection, but some sorrow
For though I've seen them pass today,
Will they come again tomorrow?

Not Going for a Walkie
with Corkey the Yorkie

Corkey the Yorkie won't go for a walkie

He sits in his basket, and with eyes like a
hawk

he stares, and curls up immobile in bed

As if to go anywhere fills him with dread.

Corkey the Yorkie – he does like to barkie

Much better than going for a walk in the
parkie

Corkey the Yorkie won't play with the
ballie

And nor will be listen to you when you
callie.

Corkey the Yorkie – he does love his
dinner,

No worries that he's going to get any
thinner.

Ah! Corkey the Yorkie is getting more perky

His behaviour's becoming decidedly quirky.

Who's that in the garden that's chasing the
cat?

Lawks – it's our Corks! What is he playing at?

Corkey the Yorkie has found his true forte

And just how much fun it can be to be
naughty …

And what could be better than that?

Labrador

Everyone loves the affable lab
Cheerful, joyful, seldom sad
Clears table-tops with a sweep of his tail
In a flash he's emptied the garbage pail.

Some say owning a lab is a doddle
He wants so much to get it right
But there's nothing this canine bin won't
snaffle
(He's even been known to down a
falafel)
And get so big he can scarcely waddle.

So be sure to keep him trim –

Take him for a swim.

With a flying leap he's into the water

No gingerly putting a toe in the edge.

And he takes a flying leap at life,

Whole-hearted, not just a half or

quarter.

Your lovely lab may be pure gold

But when he's rolled

In something revolting

Come heat, come cold,

It's out with the hose

And then a good dousing

Before he's back in the fold.

Where are the Poodles?

There are oodles of doodles,
Labradoodles (any food'll doodle),
Golden Doodles, Irish Doodles,
Dalmadoodles too
There are oodles of doodles,
But where are the poodles?

Cock-a-doodle-doo,
Or should that be cockapoo?
Cockapoo, jackapoo, cavapoo,
You could fill zoos with 'poos,
There are oodles of doodles,
But where are the poodles?

Charlie, Freddy & Bill

It's easy to give them those
sausagey names
With their little long bodies
and tiny wee legs
but there's much more to
dachshunds
than just to compare them
With something to go with
fried bacon and eggs.

Charles Chipolata's
folk came from Italia;
He has velvety ears
and the softest brown eyes.
Though not sporty,
he's fittish
And even quite skittish,
'Now I'm naturalised British,
Though once I was foreign,'
he sighs.

Fred Frankfurter's German
He can preach quite a sermon
On his friends and the badgers
they hunt.
He's bigger and stronger
And – naturally – longer
Than Charlie, who's mini
Though not, I'd say, skinny
And Charlie is nobody's runt.

Bill Banger's not skittish and nor
is he fittish.
Rather he's fattish and definitely
British
You'll find him all over, north,
south, east and west
At breakfasts and barbecues
loved by the guests.

Charles Chipolata
Though small, has a heart a
Lion would be proud to own.
Big Billy Banger can always be
trusted
Cheery, solid, and not one to
moan.
Strong Fred loves his cousins
For though they may vary,
(Some smooth and some hairy,)
They're all of them dachses –
jawohl!

41

Little Dog Leaping in the Long Long Grass

Little dog leaping in the long long grass

Now he's hidden, now he bounces,

Sees a bee and quickly pounces

Jack-in-the-box in the dandelion clocks

Up and down in the tall green grass

Little dog flying through the crisp brown leaves,

Helter-skelter, somersaulting

Round and round, and never halting

Twigs snapping, dog yapping,

Twisting, leaping, flying in the dry brown leaves.

Little dog rolling in the frost-sharp grass,

Feels the prickles on his skin

The cold is like a sharp new pin

Grunting with delight, squinting in the light,

Little dog squirming in the ice-cold grass

Little dog snuffling in the
green spring grass
Sniffs the freshness in the air
Scent of rabbit, fox and hare
Spring is now and summer's
near
Once more to be leaping in the
long long grass.

Poor Little Rich Dog

My name is Bill and I live on the streets,

They call me a rough sleeper

But I'm not alone for I have Fred

He's a human and I'm his keeper.

I hear there are dogs who live in warm houses,

And don't do a thing all day long.

They have warm feather beds

Where they lie and they sigh

And they cry for companions like Fred.

Poor sad lonely dogs, and how lucky I am

To spend all day long with my Fred

Sometimes we're cold but I could have been sold

To a rich busy owner and never have known a

Life with such faithful friends.

So please don't feel sad for
rough sleepers like us.
With Fred and our friends we
get plenty of fuss.

One day, Fred says, he'll have
his own place

But only if I can come too.

Don't separate us from those
whom we love

I'd rather be cold and not have
enough

Than eat pheasant alone in a
palace.

To a Sleeping
Tibetan Terrier Puppy

Raggedy impish rug of black curls
Is there a dog in there?
Sometimes the glimpse of little pink tongue
Or the tiny white teeth of the still very young
Suggests there's a dog in there.

As I look on the floor at this length of shag pile –
There can't be a dog in there –
I see at one end the hint of a tail wag
And a ripple of breath runs through the black
shag …
There could be a dog in there.

I tiptoe my way through the half-open door
Leaving this mass of inanimate hair,
And when I return there are feathers galore
A ripped open cushion, a vase on the floor
And a small flying whirlwind of glossy
black curls –

Oh yes, there's a dog in there!

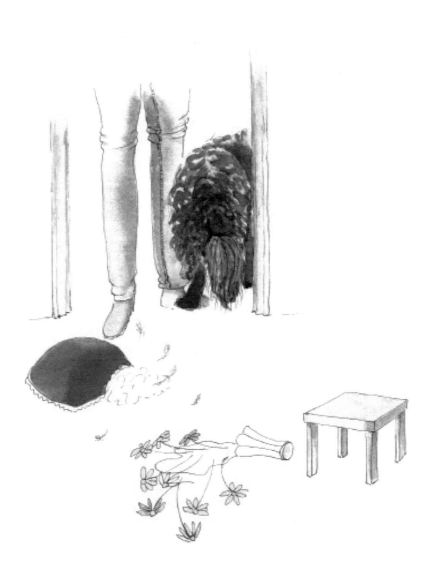

The Other Side of Dolly

A little border terrier came to
live with us,
Sad, homesick and unsettled
but oh so very sweet.

'Leave me alone, I don't want
your fuss.'
So we loved her, walked her,
fed her,
And let her find her feet.

Slowly she responded to our
care,
And soon she dared to curl up
on my chair

No longer lost and alone – rather the dog
with the bone,
A little dog with attitude
Always funny, sometimes good.

Things changed, and Dolly
couldn't stay.
She left us on a bright spring
day,
She, sad, bewildered, not to
blame,
I, her Judas, filled with shame
For I had let her down.

Back home, the days seemed
long and grey,
No balls to throw, no games
to play
Since Dolly went away.

But things in life don't stay the
same
and Dolly's found another
home
She's safe and loved
and understood,
Our terrier with attitude.

The sun still shines, the bees
still hum
The other side of Dolly
And I can laugh, no longer
numb
With grief at Dolly's going,

But sometimes when I'm in the park
I see a little Border playing –
His bright bright eyes and short
sharp bark;
My heart leaps back six months or
more
To Dolly waiting by the door
The little dog who stayed a while
The little dog who made us smile,
And brought joy into our lives.

Boxer

Bouncy, boisterous, bossy boxer,

My athlete with the squashy nose

I love to watch his flying leaps

He seems to be on springs,

Reaching ever further

Like flying without wings.

SDM
2021

And I love to watch him sleeping,
Sometimes twitching as he dreams,
Snuffling though comatose
The active sportsman in repose
My lovely, bouncing, happy boxer
My athlete with the squashy nose.

Parson Jack Russell

They named me after a parson
But it isn't because I'm good;
I go where I want and I do what I like,
Not what I ought or I should.

How Those Dogs Move!

Dotty dalmatians dance
And – usually in France –
Posh poodles parade and prance
While cockapoos captivate with a single glance.

Deerhounds dazzle with their impressive height
Fox terriers frolic, or for fun take flight.
Pekingese perambulate as if they had all day
From dawn to dusk, however, Parson Russells only
play.

Collies crouch or even creep
Upon their unsuspecting sheep
While boxers bounce and chihuahuas charm
Dandies with their topknots know just how to disarm.

Long-striding lurchers lope with easy grace,
Greyhounds get cracking – there's a hare to chase.
While Maltese make merry with ribbons in their hair
And a cuddly Bernese puppy got mistaken for a bear.

While whippets whizz and Salukis sprint,

Clumbers lumber and handsome pointers point.

Beardies beguile us with their flowing locks

And cherished crownéd corgis command the royal box.

These are a mixture of canines small and large,

Each one designed to fulfil a certain charge.

But here is a mystery that's worthy of a blog,

How does each one know that the other is a dog?

Milly Sniffalot
& Molly Scoffalot

When can we go for a walkie?
I need to have a good sniff
Who's been walking on our road today?
Who has left us a clue?
This is our gossip column and all that you
read is true:

Merry the terrier stopped by this tree;
Regal the Beagle came by this fence.
And Besty the Westy was sniffing the gutter
(Young Besty is owned by a good-natured nutter
And he does let him have a good sniff).

Not like Lottie the Scottie who's chivvied along
By someone who never has time
'Come along Lottie, I've phone calls to make
Hurry now, Lottie I've six cakes to bake.'
For her, sniffing's a serious crime.

Ringer the Springer – he's certain to come.
And Ringer's old bloke – he does like a
smoke,
So Ringer can linger – no need to rush home.
I'm Milly Sniffalot, I live on this street,
I know every inch for it's long been my beat.

One of my neighbours is little round Molly
She's lived here for years and she's really quite jolly.
She's taught her owner she must rest her feet
Though she will carry on after getting a treat.
From the fence to the tree and then her feet ache

So she simply must have a mini treat break.
From the tree to the pond and then her feet fail
'I need some refreshment – I feel rather pale.'
She's Molly Scoffalot and she lives near here.

Her friend's Zip-it the Whippet;

they make a strange pair.

When in the park they meet

Barry the Harrier;

He likes to race Zip-it

(though he's never won).

Sometimes Happy the Papillon

joins in the fun,

And Zip-it goes mad when

he can't get a run.

When Molly's not scoffing

and Milly's done sniffing

Milly and Molly both have a spiffing

Time sharing the news they have learnt.

From them nothing's hidden, though

betrayal's forbidden,

So they'll never tell and we'll never hear

Those secrets that Milly and Molly

hold dear.

Chart Topper – Le Bulldog

A plump little Frenchman is topping the charts
He's ousting lab, yorkie and cockapoo
How has he captured all those British hearts?
And right in the middle of Brexit too!

Monsieur has developed a fine line in snoring
As well as in panting, snuffling and sniffling.
But his owner says, 'My dog's never boring'
And any annoyance is merely trifling.

I'm told ce petit cost a great deal of money
But his fans say he's worth every euro.
From the time he arrives he's unfailingly funny
It's laughter each day with their little hero.

They couldn't care less he's a couch pomme de terre
In fact it's all part of his gallic charm.
And when you leave him he turns not a hair,
As long as he's comfortable, cosy and warm.

My Collie, My Lovely

My collie, my lovely
My beauty with the shining eyes,
Who watches me from where he lies
Gaze unblinking,
Always thinking
Ready and waiting when I arise.

By far the brightest of the pack
Coat of white and glossy black
Crouches down low
Heeds the signal to go
One jump ahead, always on track.

He's smartypants and clever clogs,
Shows up all the other dogs
Clever and quick,
Never misses a trick
Watchfully waiting – still as a log.

And even when he's dreaming

In his sleep he goes on scheming.

When I see his twitching muzzle,

He's not counting sheep, he's solving

a puzzle

But one word from me – he's
right there at my knee,
So loyal, so lovely, my collie,
my beauty.

Glen

Glen was a collie who came here to stay,
A young dog away for the first time from home,
(He'd heard the expression, that
'when in Rome' …)
So wanted to do things the proper way.

What should he do in this house?
We don't take food from the table
Or hang around waiting for treats,
But when you are good
You may get a reward
Though nothing that's chocolatey,
sickly or sweet.

He followed me round, picking up clues,
His brain never still, his eyes to me glued
The perfect house guest so keen to do well,
And fit in however he could.

He slept in the kitchen at home
But here he followed me up to my room
He settled at once and started to doze
(Though in the night I fancy he crept
To press his soft nose to my face as I slept).

Last thing before sleeping, I knelt down to pray,

And left him to snooze in the place where he lay.

When I opened my eyes and turned round to look

He sat there beside me, front paws on the bed,

For in this house you can go upstairs,

In this house you can lie on chairs,

In this house you should say your prayers

Before you go to bed.

So when I took him home, I said,

'Glen sat to say his prayers'; they said

'In this house we don't kneel to pray,

But Glen knows that when he's away

There are house rules he must obey

And one is bedtime prayers'.

Lovely, clever, watchful Glen,

I'm so glad you came to stay again.

Though never again, it must be said,

Did you say your prayers before going to bed!

The Good, The Bad
& The Restoration

Good, good staffie, gentle,
clever, loyal dog,
Nursemaid, guardian of the
home
The children loved and
trusted you;
And you never ever let them
down,
And if they did neglect you,
as young children sometimes
do
Your sweet stout heart was
guaranteed to stay faithful
and true.

Bad, bad staffie, savage,

dangerous, vicious dog

Taught to bite, attack or maim

Hated, feared, held in

contempt,

Though you were not the one

to blame.

Beaten from the start, you

never stood a chance,

Sweetness turned to anger,

softness to defiance.

Poor, poor staffie, but please
don't you despair
We can restore that damaged
life
With kindness, love and
patient care.
We won't let those who beat
you have the final voice,
You'll be again what you once
were,
And then we'll all rejoice.

Farewell

I don't miss all those vets' bills; they could be quite a
strain
Or walking late at night in the cold and pouring rain.
I don't have to rush now to be back here for you,
Or plan my days around you in the way I used to do.

No more ringing Petpals – can you help me please?
Or taking you to kennels (though you trotted off with
ease)
Or worry when we're walking and a dog comes into sight
Knowing that you never could resist starting a fight.

Life is so much simpler, more convenient than ever
Choosing when to rise and when to walk and when to go
to bed
But all these things, they weigh but just a fraction of a
feather
While losing you, and all you mean, weigh like a ton of
lead.

About the Author

Gail Halley has loved dogs ever since she was presented with a Sealyham Terrier puppy on her fourth birthday (many decades ago).

When not able to have her own dog she sometimes looked after other people's, and for a number of years was a foster carer with Dogs' Trust.

She has written poems – mainly light-hearted – over about 15 years when amused or inspired by the many and varied dogs she has known, all part of God's wonderful creation.

It was only when someone asked her if she had published that the idea entered her head, and it came to fruition when – unexpectedly – she linked up with Sue, and with her beautiful illustrations suddenly that idea became a possibility.

About the Illustrator

Illustration is a new discipline of art for Sue, who has been working for the last 30 years in botanical, animal and wildlife art - exhibiting, tutoring and working on commissions.

Sue's venture into art only began when she and her husband, Mike, and two daughters moved to England. With the art experience gained, Sue was ready to try this new field of illustration and seized the opportunity when her friend and author, Gail, mentioned wanting to publish her poems with illustrations.

Since childhood in Cape Town, South Africa, Sue has had a love of art and started drawing at an early age. However, any form of art education proved elusive and so she pursued her other interest, that of medical science, and obtained a B.Sc. degree at the University of Cape Town.

. . .

...

It was while working in medical research in Jerusalem that Sue first became acquainted with the author, Gail, who was working at Christ Church.

Now both living in England, they have kept in touch over the years and in 2020 entered into a collaboration for this book.

Sue's two daughters, Sarah and Jane (Positive Poetry), have worked together to create the final publication.

More Titles from Positive Poetry

Was | Is | Always - Prayer Poems By Rosanna Altman

In Other Words [zine] - Anthology of hope poetry

The End of Me, The Beginning of You - By Chloe Mae

What if? - By Janey McLeod-White

www.positivepoetry.org